I WON'T BE WEARING A BIKINI, BUT I'M GOING TO KEEP ON SWIMMING

A STORY OF COLON CANCER SURVIVAL

LORRAINE BALCH LIMERO

Kravitz & Sons

INNOVATORS IN PUBLISHING, MARKETING AND ADVERTISING

Kravitz and Sons LLC
204 E Arlington Blvd. Suite B
Greenville, NC 27858

Published by Kravitz and Sons LLC.
ISBN: 979-8-89639-657-4 (sc)
ISBN: 979-8-89639-656-7(e)

Library of Congress Control Number: 2026905624

Because of the dynamic nature of the Internet, any web addresses or links contained in this book may have changed since publication and may no longer be valid. The views expressed in this work are solely those of the author and do not necessarily reflect the views of the publisher, and the publisher hereby disclaims any responsibility for them.

ACKNOWLEDGEMENTS

For Elizabeth and Audrey, for Jay and Snoopy's creator... your stories gave me courage I could only have imagined.

For Dr S. (1941-2003)...something so gossamer connects my soul to yours that I will know you in Paradise.

Table of Contents

Introduction

"Pain skewers my eyes shut

Drifting up from no man's land

A bee left in a hive

Workers swarm around

Keeping me viable

I had cancer yesterday

Now I am clean

Berthed in intensive care

Gutted, trussed like a turkey

Bandaged up

Hopeful

AND THEN IT RETURNS"

The "Saturday Night Live" alumna Gilda Radner said of the cancer that later claimed her life, "It's one of the most unfunny things that anyone could have." Yet Gilda's story was replete with humor —it's often impossible to separate the tragic from the comedic. She handled her tragedy with so much grace—laughter, of course, is the natural analgesic.

Researchers indicate that between 7 and 9 percent of all adults will contract colon cancer at some point in their lives. Benign polyps in first-degree relatives increase risk by 74 percent for their children and siblings. A colonoscopy is a relatively pain-free procedure. I was so very fortunate to have a favorable outcome despite my own rationalizations that seriously delayed treatment.

FALLING INTO
the DEEP END

Physically prepped and emotionally primed for my first colonoscopy, I cut the tension with humor. "If I'm going to be on television today, could I ask for a "stunt double"?

At the age of 50, I'm still into magical thinking. Calamities happen to others. But, why should I expect to be blessed with health at every turn as if I'm a superior human being?

I'd done a satisfactory job blaming my symptoms on less innocuous conditions like hemorrhoids or colitis. But, in the end, it was difficult to ignore the positive hemocult and the doctor's urgency that "we do something about this immediately."

I wasn't even in a "risk" group — cancer hasn't been in my family for generations. I don't smoke. I may have a few glasses of wine a year. I eat my broccoli.

Drifting to consciousness through the anesthesia, I'm tethered out in space. I struggle to focus on something familiar. I feel isolated and concerned. I need some reassurance. Where are the nurses who will tell me everything is normal? They arrive but the news isn't good. I have a mass of 4-5 cm.

"I'm so sorry," says one of the nurses eventually as I become more aware of my surroundings and my situation. Her demeanor seems awkward and a bit evasive...who could ever enjoy relating bad news? I feel as if she's wielded a sledge hammer and it's just made contact with my gut.

The gastroenterologist meets with my husband, Tom. He is gallant and kind and tries to soften the blow. "The growth appears cancerous." (I think it looks like the Goodyear blimp.)

Little did I know that I was in for a roller coaster ride alternating between bouts of euphoria and discouragement for several years.

Tom has adopted the role of "wait and see." I marvel at his optimism as I think of his parents, who both died of cancer well before they could enjoy retirement.

He says, "You know, Lorraine, we are going to get through this." And I try so desperately to believe Tom.

My husband, my lover, my friend...how did a naive young woman of twenty whose heart was captured that quickly find someone who was so good for her soul? He is, literally, the answer to my prayer.

Tom has an important business trip. We strive for normalcy, and he leaves for London while I await the preliminary pathology —a long three days.

Boundless joy – the biopsies show no malignancy. I keep the message on my answering machine for three days, savoring the good news. I celebrate winning the lottery. I call overseas to wake Tom.

But I am struck by a virulent lethargy – I am walking around with a dentist's lead apron. I fear I am hemorrhaging. It turns out that my red blood cell count is normal.

This isn't my style, but I scan the hallways at work for a resting spot just to "catch a few."

It's All About Sinking
or Swimming

"The day I was diagnosed with cancer

I stood outside myself in denial

Battery acid in my mouth

Hot tears stain my cheeks

I was jerked back to reality

By a barrage of invasive tests after"

A week later, I am consulting with Dr. S, a surgeon, who has been heartily recommended by the medical community. I trust him when he connects with me emotionally. He discusses procedures A-Z even though I don't want to think about X, Y, and Z. The tumor is part of the colon wall. It will be a difficult surgery with so little room for resecting and for the first time, the word "colostomy" is mentioned.

I beseech God. I rail, "I need more time to tidy up my life."

I begin obsessing about worst-case outcomes and mentally plan my own funeral. I believe in living memorials. I am adamant about cremation. I catastrophize and become emotionally labile. I am buoyed by humor and seek out friends who can make me laugh. I visit the chapel at work daily. Thank you, God, for giving this to me and sparing someone I love...I can handle it.

I knew better than to ask God to zap away my tumor...I don't believe that he works in mysterious ways like that. Rather, I pray that He will help me to handle whatever comes my way.

I do some of my best work as a therapist. I have so much energy but there's a giddiness to it...I hope my patients don't pick up on this. I am unraveling. At my request, one of my colleagues prescribes some glue...a low dose of Valium.

Kyle, my 16-year old has just won the high school science fair. He's about to receive honors from a group of meteorologists at the local FOX affiliate. All I can think about is that I'm going to die (soon, but probably, safe to say, not this evening at the station). I chew a Valium since I don't have access to a water fountain and the ruminations quit for a while. With a little help I can focus on something other than my crisis.

Day one. more prep. At times I am drinking the equivalent of Galveston Bay—only slightly less noxious.

I meet a nurse who will be my guardian angel on this journey. Quieting my panic, Susie tells me that I have not signed any release today for resecting the colon. My surgeon will try to remove the tumor with a scope. Susie restores my confidence. I won't have to worry about having a colostomy today.

At 5 a.m. I awake to my first conscious thought, "the Lord has made this day...rejoice and be glad in it." This comes to me like a special gift. I have a talisman to carry into surgery.

Tom kisses my cheek. His hand slips from mine. I'm rolled away.

The anesthesiologist tries several exploratory sticks at my veins before finding success and I am asleep before I arrive in the operating room.

An hour later, gravelly from the airway, I ask, "Is the tumor gone?"

No, but I am scheduled for abdominal surgery tomorrow. I'll be opened like some birthday package—with any luck, my surgeon will be like my father who respects every inch of ribbon and gift wrap, wasting nothing. This must represent a holdover from the Depression for my dad.

Roman civilizations could predict the future in a pile of warm entrails...what will my gut portend?

Help Me, I Don't Know
How *to* Swim

I need to apologize to my family. I want to protect them from all of this. It's not fair to them.

Since my wedding more than 25 years ago, I have not deliberately worn white. Hospital garb is itself depressing. I could use something beguiling with shoulder pads. I have difficulty recognizing myself in the mirror... I look so lost.

I have two antibiotic enemas scheduled. The first one doesn't take. I've been assaulted too much today, and my body won't cooperate. The errant plastic tubing soaks my bed with antibiotics, and I shiver while the nurses change my linens.

Dr. S visits me at 9:30 the next morning. I remark on how gifted he is.

He answers by saying, "So is a mechanic."

"But, I need you today... My car is running well."

A wise nurse tells me to think of the cancer as the infection and the chemo as the antibiotic.

Nurse Susie comes by to check on me —she responds well to my radar and bouts of feeling sorry for myself. With her divine sense of knowing what is important, she allows me to cry on her shoulder. I ask whether she can scrounge around for a Bible.

The next morning, she returns with her own and writes a loving dedication to me about faith and hope.

I'm back in the "holding tank" of pre-op. There are about ten other androgynous patients here playing the waiting game —every one of them looking like some disembodied head bobbing on a sea of sterility.

I look longingly at the man who seems to have an IV bag full of pina coladas. I think he's going to lose a kidney today.

I want the staff to know I don't have Munchausens syndrome— hanging out in pre-op is not my style. After several uncomfortable jabs, I have an epidural started —this will provide pain relief for the beginning stages of recovery. I'm anesthetized before I'm taken to surgery.

Awakening with all the trappings of major surgery, I ask the recovery room staff, "Any cancer in the frozen section?" "No cancer." I will always believe there was a host of angels in the operating room.

I am receiving fluids and massive antibiotics through a subclavian. A Foley carries away urine. An "NG" (nasogastric) tube rubs my throat raw and drains out stomach contents to give my gut a rest. In a moment of surrealism, I think about the unwitting war casualty in *Catch- 22* being warehoused with a self-contained loop between elimination and nourishment. I am alert but sleepy.

I quickly learn to master the joystick that feeds extra Demerol through my IV. I wonder whether this skill would make me a more competitive "Jeopardy" contestant. For the most part, the epidural keeps me nearly pain-free.

Dr. S relates that he has never done a resection with so little room to spare. My colon is held with staples. I bless him for his genius. He remains modest.

My fever spikes to 101. Some Tylenol now flows through the tangle of plastic tubing.

My children take turns sponging my back. For me, their tenderness is glorious payback given the thousands of diaper changes I've made over the past 26 years! I revel in their instinctive gestures to comfort and console. With my hugs and kisses I blotted so many of the tears that spilled on their silky baby skin. They have returned the caring commensurately.

I am asked to cough frequently and take deep breaths. I'm grumpy today.

There is a general euphoria among staff when my gut comes alive with gas three days after surgery. If I succeed with flatulence management, I'll probably be getting an A+ in post-op. This will require some finesse — I'm afraid I'll blow out my staples. Ever polite, it's difficult for me to follow the request to "let 'em rip."

I'm not getting enough sleep. My roommate's boyfriend is boarding with us...he's the one on the floor by her bed ...the snoring is cacophonous and messes with my circadian rhythms. This invasion is unwelcome.

Shortly after the "snorer" makes his farewells, Sylvia, a nurse buddy from psychiatry, comes by to say hello. For years now she's been a confidante of sorts, and I adore her funny bone. I know she's well-intended with her gift of glazed doughnuts, but I still look at her with disbelief. How am I going to reverse peristalsis with this NG tube and suck up some crumbs? Alas, my family gets to scarf them up.

It's been five days since I've washed my oily hair. I'm looking more like a brunette than a blond. I think my vanity is a good sign.

I am physically hampered with technology and manage to turn myself into a pretzel with the bed controls.

Six days without food —my children are puzzled and wonder why I'm not hungry. Through the IV I've probably consumed enough calories to fuel a team of sled dogs for the Alaskan Iditerod.

The NG tube will go this morning. This feels like real progress. With a few exploratory tugs, I'm now ambiguous about whether to keep it after all. It's really made me look too sickly, but I think ripping it out of my gullet will smart. Whoa, I'm being whip lashed through the first ring of hell and back and I've mauled the nurse's forearm in my frenzy. But, when the ride is over, the relief is fabulous.

I am now receiving "prn" (shorthand for an "as requested" dose rather than a set dose) morphine for pain control. I ask only once. I have my dad's recuperative powers.

Dr. S has the final pathology report. The cancer is encapsulated in the tumor. The wall of the colon surrounding the mass is clear, and there's no lymph node involvement.

"Stage One" in medical vernacular. I do not need either radiation or chemo.

On day 7, Dr. S removes the thirty or so staples from my abdomen. The incision extends from my waist in a southerly direction for about 8 inches to "kingdom come," detouring around my navel.

Day 8, I'm ready for discharge. The subclavian line is the last conduit to go. I must remain flat on my back for 40 minutes to allow for clotting. Ever ready to push the envelope of imagination, I have visions of St. Sebastian's beatific face as he spurts blood in his martyrdom.

Just Barely *Treading* Water

Homecoming—a humid, hard-to-catch-your-breath morning. I feel frail and raw. My tears are never far away and I use them for a good cleansing.

Two weeks after surgery, I have my first checkup with Dr. S. My son, Christopher, in a gallant show of support, offers to escort me in his beloved (and showroom perfect) Mustang. I decided to have fun with him. "I haven't been incontinent for several days... Thanks. It shouldn't be a problem." Fortunately, he's used to my rather irreverent sense of humor.

A psychotherapist of many years, I have regarded myself as an emotional healer. Now, it's my turn to reach out for help through the services at M.D. Anderson Hospital, one of the premier cancer treatment facilities. A survivor with a similar surgical history telephones. She offers me hope.

But doubt, like an errant BB in one of those plastic puzzles, seeks purchase—is it truly gone?

The greatest challenge of this recovery is teaching my colon to work again. I have forgotten a few steps of that exquisite tango "peristalsis."

I learn to appreciate that which I had taken for granted and nearly lost. I am weary but radiant. For now I'll revel in being alive.

Wanting to return a long overdue thanks to a physician co-worker for giving me a friendly shoulder "to cry on," I pick up a well-rounded peach pie from the bakery and drive to his office as soon as I have the green light from Dr. S to get behind the wheel. (It's a marvel that I can drive this soon after being flayed open!)

Nibbling at the crust, I muse, "This really could have been bad.

To which he responds, "It was bad."

Maybe I'm taking this too lightly. It is still not real to me.

Several months after surgery, I dissociated during an invasive checkup. My modesty is surprisingly intact. (I thought that I had lost all sense of decorum after the birth of my third child). I am handed a drape that has a large round opening—this can't be good—and, as I kneel into a table that tilts me into an awkward position, Dr. S checks the site of the resection. I am blessed with good news. Everything there looks clean as a "whistle, spic 'n span."

I breeze through other checkups effortlessly. It seems the cancer has eventually become just a footnote to my life.

I am deeply touched when a friend visiting in the Holy Land invokes my name at the Wailing Wall. These prayers are good. I am flying with God's radar!

Chris weds his love of many years in the spring. We bask in their adoration for each other. I am smug as I brush the soft folds of the fuchsia silk dress that hugs my shoulders. "Not bad for a mother-in-law!"

Shortly after the wedding, I sign up and "run" in a local "Relay for Life" event to benefit the Cancer Society, believing everyone else more deserving of the applause from the cheering bystanders. I've linked arms with friends who have battled prostate cancer and breast cancer. We try to sprint around the track.

I'm convinced the "affinity for chocolate" nodule situated at the foot of the colon that I've just had removed is gone for all time. Like those etchings in early medical texts that draw and quarter the torso in a macabre way, I can imagine that part neatly snipped.

My exuberance at the good checkups is tempered by the nagging reality that I am still in the bathroom up to 20 times a day, plagued by the pressure to relieve myself but with negligible results. At times, it seems as if I am sloughing off bloody tissue and little else.

I have to rely on stimulants for results. I consult with Dr. M., my gastroenterologist, during the year, but, despite my misgivings, all tests appear encouraging.

Months later, Tom and I plan an impulsive trip to Japan. Not wanting to ruin a bit of this interlude, I don't complain that during much of the fourteen-hour flight I'm in excruciating pain. In retrospect, I believe I was sitting on the tumor.

The scenery is idyllic. In Nikko at the shrine of the Shogun, I waft delicious incense into my face and clap my hands to summon the Deity. "Please let the cancer be gone." I take comfort in speaking to God in different ways. In the idyllic serenity of this mountain village, I begin reading the teachings of Buddha.

I receive one of the most potent life lessons from an unlikely source while vacationing in Japan. Queuing up in a line at the information kiosk in the underground station, I am fascinated by a rather industrious elderly man "policing" the turnstile.

Absorbed in his task, he displays an air of confidence and efficiency as he lifts dirt from the grid and polishes the rubber surface. For him, this is the most important job in the world and being in his orbit, I agree.

I walk away feeling elevated and take this lesson to heart. If I ever catch myself hiding out in that "ivory tower" of smugness that's about having a "Master's degree," I can recall this dose in humility for self-leveling.

I have to push myself way beyond my limits to keep up with Tom's agenda. I get exhausted easily and sweat so that a crust of salt accumulates on my temples. If not for Tom's prodding, I'd still be sitting on my suitcase in that labyrinth under Tokyo Station, crying into my shoes.

Dr. S orders some labs —a "CEA" (known as a carcinogenic embryonic antigen test) that checks for markers indicative of tumor activity, and a metabolic panel that monitors liver function. There will also be a repeat colonoscopy. (You really need to know the lingo to be a bona fide member of the program.)

I report to radiology for a chest x-ray and CT scan of the pelvis. If colon cancer metastasizes the tumors typically spread to the liver or lungs. The tests themselves are not nearly as daunting as waiting for the results. Fear—real and imagined—ratchets up.

I'm sure I'm not ingratiating myself to my friends through this fretting. But, with sublime patience, they let me vent. If I feel compelled to say something 1000 times, they graciously listen.

I resort again to humor as I report today on the surgery for the colonoscopy. I sport a racy tattoo on my right buttock. It's a rather perky-breasted "she devil." I think I'm a hit! I'm sure Dr. M has never seen the like!

I fortify myself with the thought, "If they find anything, it'll be so tiny, they can snip it off easily."

But, oh, déjà vu. Same dirge, next verse. I'm so afraid. Once again, the nursing staff keeps their distance, and I am left alone to assimilate the awful news that the tumor has come back. We pick up the emotional pieces with Tom's solid optimism.

Though I face another questionable prognosis, I am somehow reassured by Dr. M's kindly demeanor. He is a "gentle" man and seems invested in accompanying me on this journey in which I often appear to have lost my way.

For weeks I hang out in movie theaters, choosing the especially sad films to give me an excuse for tears. I sob my way through the summer's blockbusters, seriously waterlogging my popcorn. I try so hard not to cry in front of my children.

Not one to believe in pure coincidence, I find deliberateness in my daughter's leaving correspondence to a friend in plain view. She is my scared little girl as she pours out her fears and apprehensions by speculating about whether I might die. The pathos of that discovery makes me wish that I could reassure Rachel with confidence, "I'll beat this." I do my best not to exacerbate her fear.

Though it's actually a short interval until we have a game plan for my second surgery, I feel time is somehow distorted. Things run counter to all logic.

I am terribly nauseous. After a few weeks of this, I figure it's not worth it to eat, and I begin to lose weight.

I arrive early in the morning for my CT scan. I must be depleted…I'm learning to sleep sitting up. During my nap, a caring radiology clerk found a blanket for my shoulders. It's small gestures like this that truly humble me. I huddle, looking like ET.

The scan itself is surprisingly anticlimactic. Two cocktails that are basically drinkable will make my insides more photogenic. I have a bumpy ride as the table jerks me along like it has a defective conveyor belt. Neither test shows evidence of malignancy.

I check in with Dr. S to review possible procedures. The likely surgery will include a colostomy (my rectum will be removed, and the opening will be sutured.) The remaining length of bowel will be brought to the surface of my abdomen and stitched in place. A lot of this goes right over my head.

Understandably, I become possessive of that oft-maligned body part, imagining it winking in a jar of preservative in some dusty pathology lab. Or will it be unceremoniously cast upon the pyre of discarded body parts? It appears I don't have a say-so in this matter.

I don't want to feel scared, so my "shtick" shifts into overdrive. "It will just be decorative now," I muse, "like a porcelain sculpture."

In a nostalgic vein, I quip, "People don't appreciate their assholes enough."

Being a respectful surgeon, he meets me exactly where I need to be. "Women do..." (long pause for effect), "They tend to marry them."

He wants to see the tumor for himself, and it is situated so very close to the anus that the options are fairly limited. There's still a huge theme here...this won't happen to me.

This is a jewel of a day, and here I am faced with news that could change my life forever.

Fear is a metallic taste in my mouth. I find myself still rearranging the facts to negotiate a different outcome. If I hadn't eaten so much red meat...

The odds against a recurrence were actually quite high.

With the news that I am "going under the knife" again, I am ready to relegate my journal to the heap. My optimism is degenerating, and the notion of "happily ever after" is a mockery. In my self-pity, I feel cheated of that good prognosis.

I leave the office asking for a hug and with a referral for a second opinion. I have a tentative date for surgery in about 10 days.

For a while I've been feeling like a lemon...the rundown car that needs all this expensive attention when you bring it to the mechanic. "This is gonna go in a coupl'a thousand miles, lady... this gizmo is all shot..." And so, "it was," in a manner of speaking, as I ventured out for a second opinion.

Out in Rough *Waters*

Dr. B. my "second opinion" surgeon is one of the very best colorectal specialists in the city. Having operated on an ex-president and several other world leaders, he comes with an excellent pedigree.

Not prepping in advance for his exam, I'm subjected to the medical version of water blasting. Since he was on the receiving end of the rather unpleasant hydraulics, I didn't begrudge his substantial fees. I feel like a science fair project gone terribly wrong.

I am reminded of my newborn daughter, bare under the bilirubin lights, and of how vulnerable she must have seemed to all the folks who came to the hospital nursery to witness her debut. She looked so much cuter in this position than I do.

He takes some generous biopsies and has to use silver nitrite to cauterize all the rawness. It is painful and an assault to my dignity despite the staff's professionalism.

Dr. B concurs with all the exams, but the game plan he proposes is different. He recommends that I check into the hospital for more extensive tests (under anesthesia) and, pending the results, probably sign on for a course of chemo and radiation with possible resection in three months' time...or perhaps not, if the tumor doesn't shrink and all those nerves and muscles in the lower colon, that we take for granted, need to be sacrificed.

At the time, he didn't have the final pathology report from my colonoscopy.

I'm in a quandary. For God's sake, I have difficulty choosing what pair of shoes to wear. I pray. I called Dr. S and told him that I'll follow Dr. B's recommendations and will admit myself into a hospital halfway across the city. Then, I'm ashamed of being disloyal to Dr. S and ungrateful for his care.

Dr. S checks in on me with a phone call well after hours. The final pathology from the colonoscopy is in. The mass is basically a non-cancerous—an adenoma with "suspicious" cells. This means they're likely to become malignant if they have their way.

He proposes a trans-anal procedure with a scope — tricky for a surgeon, he says, but like a hemorrhoidectomy for the patient and less traumatic than abdominal-perineal surgery.

I'm praying I can avoid abdominal surgery altogether. I'm stoic. I'm ready. I can deal with this.

I rely on Tom to help me research various options. He's the Internet expert. In my negativity, I feel totally detached from any encouraging news.

Basically, the world is divided into two kinds of people —those who read the directions and those who don't. I usually dive in with bravado, figuring things out as I go, but today I'm helpless.

Blessedly, I do not remain there.

I flash back to the memory of the ballerinas in a recent production of *Dracula* as the Count devours their souls. I am being spirited across the stage like a fated lover, all but resistant to battling the machinations outside myself.

Being ill prepared for my journey, I soon learn what accoutrements I need to carry—a sense of humor, sufficient knowledge to make informed choices, a good support system, and an abiding spirituality.

I am determined not to lose "me" in the maelstrom. I have a well-honed, irreverent, often self-effacing sense of humor — the daily absurdities, the ironies of a life well lived. For me, the enormity of a genuine belly laugh is a delightful curative.

I've enrolled on a graduate-level course in a subject area I had never imagined needing. I have the syllabus in hand, and it's daunting. Through my (sometimes fanatical) grasp of the material, I'm able to reduce my anxiety level to near tolerable as I look at various options and outcomes.

The support comes en masse. My colleagues at the hospital know it is essential for me to vent, and they generously give of themselves. When I'm able to waylay a friend who will share a joke with me, so much the better. I thrive on affection and hugs. One of the psychiatrists spearheads a plan for my co-workers to wear red ribbons with angel's wings attached as a measure of their devotion. It is a beautiful gesture.

When the weight of my problems exceeds the strength of my shoulders, I utilize the opportunity to bolster my spirituality. My healing mantra becomes Psalm 121. Imagining views of verdant hills and valleys, I feel this Biblical passage gently wash over me. My grandfather was a shepherd himself, though farming was an avocation. The belief in "let go and let God" remains stalwart to this day, never wavering in the miasma of self-doubt. I am never alone.

Sometimes, at crucial events in my life, my timing has been dreadfully off. Tom is in Manchester, England, lecturing at the university and trying to keep us financially afloat. It is an obligation organized months ago.

We keep in touch as the countdown begins, amassing a huge AT & T bill.

I *Weary* of the Struggle

I check into outpatient for labs and my pre-op workup. My blood is cross-matched and typed for possible transfusion during surgery. The seriousness of my situation registers once again.

I purchase a prep kit (for cleaning things) out at the pharmacy. I'm entitled to a discount...my box is missing two sticks of dynamite!

I clock lots of bathroom hours. Before daybreak, when I'd normally be settling down for some "real" sleep, I have to wake up to finish things off with a suppository. It's a tough maneuver...it feels like someone's parked a bulldozer in my "garage."

I tart myself up with purple toenail polish and don anklets for the operating suite, thinking I'm hiding my ravaged toes —years of dancing "en pointe." After surgery, I arrived at the ICU barefoot. The mystery was cleared up upon discharge when I was handed the aforementioned items in a biohazard bag!

Chris picks me up for the early a.m. trip to the hospital. I am amazingly calm as I sit cocooned in a blanket. Strangely, I am as relaxed as I'd be chatting it up with a friend over tea.

The familiar antibiotic enema...I didn't realize that this would be the last time things would work, however marginally. I am sore, and it's tricky to bypass the tumor.

I am confident that the trans-anal procedure will be a success...that I'll be in the recovery room within a few hours with things more or less intact. I have to believe...it's a vast comfort.

My dream of having a "coven" of friends preparing me for surgery with aromatherapy, hypnosis, guided imagery, and just plain shenanigans isn't feasible. We're short on time. Instead, I have 5 minutes with Sandra, a fellow therapist, who gives me some relaxing mantras (only because she knows someone in the sacred environs of pre-op and can bully her way in. She's good at "working the room").

Basically, waiting is a solitary thing. Dr. S visits me briefly. Used to television medicine, I imagine him listening to some Boz Scaggs or Van Morrison or something equally soothing while I'm lying with my guard down and my gown open. (He doesn't seem like a heavy metal guy.)

Even so, who am I to push my agenda through at a time like this? He opts for country and western.

He looks so unsurgeon-like in his casual attire...it's like seeing God in a plaid shirt and Nikes.

But I have an abiding faith in his skill. I do believe that God placed Dr. S and other specialists in my life when I most needed them. They were heaven-sent, reassuring me and working miracles.

My calm evaporates, and I am frightened as I'm wheeled into the operating room and have to hike myself onto the table. Uneasy despite some mild medication, I try to block everything out. A dominatrix might actually enjoy implementing all this binding and immobilizing paraphernalia.

The table chillingly looks like it's a cousin to the one in the death chamber in Huntsville Prison. My arms are strapped to restraints, so I assume a crucified form, ready for the delivery of "the cocktail." Why am I compelled to gallows humor at a time like this?

Periodically, during the next five-plus hours, a weary team updates my family. The trans-anal procedure is a "no go." I require three units of packed cells due to blood loss during the abdominal perineal surgery.

I'm *Drowning*

I awake breathing into the confines of an oxygen mask with my son and daughter-in-law standing over me tenderly as if I'm some newborn in a bassinet. Gentle and tentative, they kiss my forehead. In my mind, I've never been less kissable.

They tell me that I'm sporting a sunburn without the benefit of any tropical getaway. I was in surgery; I wasn't in Hawaii. Must be something to which I'm allergic! Oh, swell, I'm not going to be photographed for *Vogue* today as I had assumed!

On some level, I had prepared myself for the colostomy. Without having to ask, I know, and the NG tube confirms the truth for me, that I've once again had extensive surgery.

I won't let on to anyone, but I don't think I can get through this.

I flash back to childbirth and the incredible fatigue of it all. "I'm outta here...I've changed my mind about this. It's too hard."

ICU is a 24-hour beehive. I know I'm receiving good care but not rest. A hospital is not the place to get rest...it's like a hive has been disturbed and all its drones are madly swarming to get to the nearest bloom before it wilts.

I'm hopeless and bereft. I doze, and in that netherworld beyond awareness, I weep.

Within hours, the blood pressure cuff that inflates on my arm with monotonous frequency leaves bruises. I'm turned on my side by two burly nurses and propped up by pillows. My organs will spill on the floor if I cooperate, and for once, I'm not sure I care about that offal possibility.

My father, who was injured in World War II when a mortar he was loading exploded prematurely, described the pain in his left buttock, "It was as if I'd been impaled on a burning axe blade."

Luckily, I'm the recipient of liberal doses of Demerol.

Charting here is electronic, and the terminal clicks nonstop outside the cubicle where I'm warehoused. I'm being dragged back to the land of the living, albeit reluctantly. I have no particular sense of time. In this way the ICU is a bit like a casino in Vegas.

I long for Tom. I long for some safety.

In that mysterious way that nature has of bringing things full circle, a former patient of mine is one of my nurses. She is a loving presence whom I came to appreciate fully months later. (At the moment I was rejecting such things, believing I was irreparably damaged—without and within.)

In my own convoluted way, I deal with this by not dealing with this. I plan to go through life without looking at "IT."

It was like being on a runaway sled plunging ever downward over the crusty snow. Experience had taught me that there were probably lots of buried rocks hidden beneath the icy coating, and I was surely doomed in the madcap dash.

There are times when I just want my company to go away. I'm not worth the salvage effort.

The next morning Dr. S makes rounds. "I forget how strong you are…what a fighter you are…I think we got it all…" Isn't that what they say 6 months before you die? I'm not buying your optimism, doctor.

I am already dead inside. I'm beyond comfort and consolation. I'm not sure why you worked so hard to save my life if this is all I'll ever be.

I'm not the least bit shy in admitting that I need my mom.

My older son Chris, who's in charge, decides that Rachel should not visit when I am at my worst. There are too many conduits in and out of my body. The monitors, oxygen masks, and drains are clearly enough for an adult to assimilate.

"I'm so sorry, baby."

Kyle, who is 17 tomorrow, is sober as he approaches my bed. If my children weren't so worried, they'd be ribbing me about the fact that I am ghostly without makeup, that I am suffering from OR hair, and that my wardrobe needs sprucing.

I wish that they could be spared from this upheaval.

Dr. H B, a dedicated friend and fellow movie buff, comes to ICU, hat in hand, with a wonderfully robust houseplant studded with silk roses...beautiful "eye candy" but a "no no" in the sterile intensive care environment. The nurses get to enjoy it instead.

I tell him I'm not winking at him—it's simply the "stun gun" fatigue that overwhelms me early on. He tries to bring me cheer, but basically, I'm just a corpse that won't be reanimated.

Tom has crossed the friendly skies despite an unfriendly ground crew in the UK whose sense of urgency in getting him home fails to match ours. This is the first time I entertain the thought that I can get through this. I begin to fight harder.

I tell Tom, "You have to be the strong one."

This seems an unfair burden when I think of it now. I won't allow him to cry.

The love of my life has taught me by example not to anticipate the worst (though I backslide on that); to revere a thing called unconditional love; to strive for greatness; and to be steadfast. We are paddling our canoe in perfect synchronicity.

Dr. S returns the next morning to tempt me with an offer. He's thinking about writing an order to have my NG tube removed. (I've been stewing in my own juices for two days now and have built up a healthy head of steam, so I become pushy with this agenda). I pursue this one like a cat to a can opener.

If there's a prayer of this, I want to get at the head of the line.

In my best intimidating tone, I bully him, "Think hard about it."

I am warned, "Not even ice chips."

If that will seal the deal, no huge sacrifice. Maybe my feistiness is good. Of course, he has the last word.

Once again, removal is vastly unpleasant but also liberating.

It's Sunday. There are too many sick people here in the ICU and I am transferred to the "Oncology Unit" by afternoon —a step up but also sobering.

I continue to repudiate my body. I could convince anyone that every molecule of my self-esteem resides in the vicinity of the stoma. I struggle to find myself.

It is today, though, that I remember my manners and thank God for bringing me this far. I have no doubt that He has been hovering above my ceiling tiles. I begin, however tentatively, to imagine a life like this.

Rescue Breathing

Shortly after ICU gives me the boot, Sharon, quite literally, waltzes into my room with a copy of *Vogue* and a hideous black feather boa that could benefit from fumigation. This is all in the name of glamour! It looks dazzling against all this hospital white and my own pallid skin. I vamp around like my bed is a stretch limo.

Sharon and I bonded immediately when she was hired as a social worker in psychiatry. She's a marvelous nurturer.

She's a cancer survivor – one of those nasty types with low cure rates. It is a blessing to know her.

Each experience she shares has all the elements of good storytelling. (She kept me enthralled once with a well-crafted account of how the ocean gradually freezes off the coast of Alaska. I never knew ice had so many permutations.)

A little sprite with blond hair darts in and out of my room and, in her wake, leaves a card with a "smiley" face. She is a tiny ambassador that brightens things for a while.

I sweat. I'm restless, and there's a burning sensation where the sheets touch my legs. I figure this is the fallout from anesthesia. The infusion pump has its own particular susurration, and its whisper becomes tattooed onto my brain.

Much to my shame, I begin to play with the thought of jumping from my 6th-story window. Thankfully, I have neither the energy nor the opportunity. I wouldn't know how. I've become one with the bed. I have a feeling that the window doesn't open anyway, just to discourage people with a like mind.

Extinguishing myself is a bad idea. I believe in life everlasting, but not if I bungle things.

I cannot rest. It's impossible to get comfortable. A stomach sleeper, I can't find an inch of skin anywhere that hasn't been sliced or fastened back together. I've been gutted like a deer. The colostomy site is raw; the incision down my belly feels like it may rip open spontaneously; and my rectum is full of stitches. I literally count the hours until dawn.

My thoughts are scrambled. I worry that I am dying. I fret most about leaving my daughter behind. The boys have the "science/math/remote gene." There's an overabundance of testosterone in this locker room...who will look out for her?

Curiosity eventually wins out, and I decide to look at "it." The clear appliance doesn't afford much of a view. Since it hasn't started working yet, it looks pretty sanitary. (I've heard there's a cow at Texas A & M that's been surgically altered with a portal so the "Ag" students can observe its digestion.) I feel about as "up front and personal."

My mind is fertile on Sunday with a kind of euphoria similar to that I had after childbirth. I have to put some meaning into this experience. After all, I have risen from the dead.

I'm holding the baton in some relay, and people are really counting on me not to stumble.

My colleagues in occupational therapy start a mini blood drive to replace the blood I've required. Having given over a gallon in another life, I feel blessed with the enormity of their gifts.

A voracious reader, I am too weak to hold even a skinny paperback for very long. This is so atypical. Like my grandmother before me, I'm not beyond reading a cereal box if nothing more stimulating is at hand.

Another puzzle... I am not hungry. This is a rare event, indeed! Amusingly, as I was being wheeled to the delivery room about to give birth for the first time 25 years ago, I was fantasizing about grabbing a tray off the rolling cart in the hallway.

"Let me tear into this Salisbury steak... the doctor's not even here yet!"

Because I can't give my hygiene more than a feeble once-over, I obsess that I stink. It's really nothing more than "hospital nose." But just to be sure, I liberally slather myself with lotion every time I work up a sweat.

My "one size fits all" gown is elephantine and slips off one shoulder. In another setting, this might be provocative. It allows for easy access and viewing. I never know when someone needs to come by for a peek.

Dr. E visits —a dear friend and colleague. Around her I feel safely swaddled. Spurred by our interest in gerontology, we talk about the Queen Mum's 100th birthday.

"I'd like to make it to my 53rd," I muse.

One of the aides is really beginning to try my patience.

Repeatedly, she asks, "Have we had a bowel movement today?" Is this something that requires a joint effort, a "we" thing? Frankly, I don't know what to expect from this colostomy. Her persistence makes me feel like I've missed the biggie on the "$64,000 Question," and I don't want to disappoint anyone with an incorrect answer.

Chris wisely brings me Barbara Barrie's book *Don't Die of Embarrassment*. I feel a kindred spirit with someone who has so profoundly affected my recovery. I greedily read for that happy ending. I am not disappointed.

Toward the end of my stay, a man with "presence" visits. He must be clergy. That's good; I need some spiritual guidance... something to anchor me. He is Tom's boss, a former astronaut, and a very approachable human being.

We talk of Tom's enthusiasm for manned space exploration and of our respective children. And, in an amazingly cavalier way, I feel the embarrassment of a gut that punctuates my comments with a huge blast of air. Not exactly a crowd-pleaser.

This is extraordinary for one who groomed herself to exercise ultimate self-control in the face of even normal, everyday personal gaffes.

I grin and say to him, "It's working well"…nice save!

I awake with the notion that clean hair is a "quality of life" issue. The culprit must be my nylon pillow. I am working on some serious dreadlocks. I'm amazed the nurses have no particular protocol for this since some oncology patients spend months here.

A new face, a Canadian nurse on the 3-11 shift, accepts the challenge. She arranges copious amounts of plastic sheeting on the mattress to allow for drainage into a wastebasket and lowers the head of the bed to further facilitate matters. I hold on for dear life like a luger about to career off course. It's heavenly and, by far, the most exciting thing that's happened today.

My room is beginning to look funereal with all these flowers—my visitors don't know that I'm really a corpse masquerading as a sick person. See this rictus!

I gauge each face for signs of pity —I'm so rejecting of myself.

I have so much admiration for my children, and that group now includes a daughter-in-law I adore. I love their ease in being communicative. With the two younger ones, things sometimes cross the bounds of good taste. (Basically, I think my parents would have been "childless" if I had ever mouthed off to that degree. But the world is more accepting now.) For once, my children are sober and uncomfortably quiet.

The world goes on outside my window.

There are few sounds more fearsome than the sirens that are amplified in the concrete abyss; that is my "Presidential suite" view.

A crew of workmen has stepped out onto the roof. They are incurious about the drama unfolding one floor below.

The grackles toss themselves on the wind like a taffeta shawl. I envy those majestic birds that easily catch the thermals. Is it really about faith? Will I learn to fly?

Through some odd juxtaposition of light, the window blinds project a "star" onto my bedspread. I am suffused with calm in the lambent light that mimics dawn.

As a rule, I have a healthy appetite. It is not unusual for me to begin salivating in anticipation of the next meal before I've even pushed away from this one. But this surgery really compromised things. Awakening on day five, I find that a liquid diet is ordered for me.

Voila! I dine Roman style —neither sitting nor supine. Between the stitches and the staples and assorted plumbing, positioning myself ladylike is an invitation to tweak the pain dial up more than a notch or two. A cup of jello, some salty bouillon... I'm full "up to here," belching and burping like I've polished off a three-star Michelin meal.

I haven't felt this smug about myself since college when I'd stretched a can of grapefruit through "breakfast, lunch, and dinner" and managed to be a size 8. My upper arm looks like it's deflated.

By lunch I've graduated to a regular diet, which, of course, is a real misnomer. Under the dome, shining like a jewel, is a gristly pattie of unrecognizable something. If I take a chance on paring it down to bite-sized kibble, I'll have to hike my leg up to anchor the plate. It looks like there's enough here to feed a platoon!

How I long for something healthy. (My first meal home was just a humble sub, but what a Technicolor wonder! My senses, long deprived, were on overload. It was probably the best meal I've ever had.)

I'm really in sync with the rhythms of this unit, and tonight I suspect that one of my fellow patients has expired. I am solemn and scared.

Most of my guests are treated to "show and tell." I need to be perfectly candid about my experience. I'm like a 3-year-old showing off her grown-up panties for the first time. If I talk of this, it validates the truth and helps me to adjust. Wrinkles, gray hair, and the diminution of physical strength are expected changes for which we prepare. This is a terrible jolt that has snuck up on me when my "pants were down."

I gave myself permission to grieve the lack of time I had to acclimate. I nurse a profound sadness.

My body has been made relatively comfortable given the circumstances, but my mind is struggling. I'm so angry that I don't want to believe in the miracle of time.

During my distress, I understand why physical pain can be a welcome distraction from emotional pain. I have empathy for my patients who have resorted to self-mutilation when thoughts and feelings become horribly unbearable. I'd rather be in excruciating physical pain than have to deal with this emotional emptiness. My spirit has been destroyed.

I received an anti-nausea drug with my IV antibiotics that really affects my sleep patterns. Awaking frequently throughout the night, unable to quiet my nervous system, I turn on the television just as the station is coming on the air. The visual is a New England-type of white clapboard church, and the background accompaniment is a lovely hymn that I used to belt out in Sunday school. Serendipity...you tell me?

If you ask me, the signs are always there. I think people tend to become jaded and stop looking at the world through eyes of wonderment. I believe in daily miracles. I cannot blame God. I need to get off the self-pity thing. Cancer is an equal opportunity illness.

Perfunctory at best, bedside baths are logistically complicated. I am a rag doll. I envy my ancestors who could at least forage for a twig to facilitate dental care. I'm still bedridden and make do with an emesis basin.

Kim, the ostomy nurse, visits to instruct me in appliance care. I size her up (which means I'm looking for the telltale bulge), thinking she's also had a colostomy. She's pretty and about 20 years younger than I am. I need assurance from her that my life can be normal again. She answers "no" to the colostomy question and patiently fields the thousand or so that follow.

She helps me peel off the plastic pouch and adhesive wafer. I saw the stoma for the first time. Dear God, it looks like I've been on the receiving end of a shotgun blast. I'm horrified by its rawness —the colon is so highly vascular. It's a gaping maw. This ghastly hole doesn't belong on my body! It's not welcome like the ten I came with.

Kim reassures me with her matter-of-fact attitude. I believe I might actually get the knack of policing up, too. She tells me that she'll return in two days to show me how to "irrigate."

As a child, I was clearly a stoic, serious kid who thought she had to soldier through even the normal bumps and bruises. To survive adulthood, I've learned to cry and to ask for help. I don't have to be protective of everyone's feelings.

Despite my smooth talk, I feel obligated to entertain my visitors. I tire so easily, and rather than chase them away myself, I wimp out and ask the nurses to post a sign on my door putting the immediate world on notice that I am sleeping. This buys me precious time to heal.

Kim shows up as planned to instruct me in the fine points of "irrigating," which is nothing more than giving yourself a daily enema to assist the colon to empty out on demand, rather than throughout the day. (Typically, the colon shuts down during slumber.)

I have to admit, I'm not taking notes. It's a Rube Goldberg kind of nightmare. My body cooperates, but my mind is light-years away, as if I'm in a quantum mechanics lecture. If I ignore this, it might go away. I have all the appeal of a ripe garbage can.

I tell Dr. S. that I don't plan to irrigate. I'll let nature "take its course" and forego the nasty process. He's respectful, and I feel like I have some control back. I win that squirmish.

The two drains sprouting from what "used to be" my anus are

a real curiosity. Dubbed "hand grenades," they seem to keep things respectable back there. Basically, I think they're attached to whatever didn't make it to pathology last week.

When Dr. S decides to tug on them a bit the day they're slated for removal, I mentally re-hem all my dresses to accommodate to their length just in case they won't budge.

Mother of God, that hurts a lot, and for a while I'm my own Greek chorus of woe and misery.

Liberated from my bed but still attached to an IV pole, I'm encouraged to "take a spin" around my room. I am so weak I lurch like a drunkard. I'm afraid I'll fall and do some serious damage. Maybe I need some training wheels.

When I advanced to a stroll out in the vicinity of the nurses' station, I noticed that the staff had installed speed bumps. Here I am at my first Indy, and already I'm yearning for the checkered flag.

It's not a pretty sight to have to drag the Foley bag with me.

I get the impression that the man in the next room is terminal. His company, which my intuition tells me are family, decide to have a "knock down, drag out." Their verbal sparring and threats have scared the pooh out of me. Since I have basic transportation now, I scoot myself and the IV pole into the restroom and lock the door for the duration of the fray. Have you ever...?

If you have to have cancer, this is probably one of the best in terms of "cure rate."

In a sense, the recurrence of the tumor was a godsend. The visible part of the mass extruding into the colon was largely benign but an indicator of something sinister and secret within, sort of like a volcano that is full of seething magma and releases only a plume of ash.

Though I carry enough weight to ever avoid looking emaciated, it's as if I'm wearing an ill-fitting coat from Goodwill. I have a saggy look.

My kidneys are working well according to the nursing scuttlebutt.

I don't mind the Foley catheter —it's the lazy man's way. It's been in place for eight days. Before I can be discharged, I have to prove to staff that I can urinate on my own after it's removed.

"Old Faithful" cooperates almost immediately. (I continue to pee in about ten different directions for a week.)

When the nurses discover that I am a psychotherapist, they lobby me to do a support group for staff once I recover. I don't envy their being in the trenches and dealing with trauma and death without a mechanism to process their feelings. "Sucking it up" on a daily basis seriously drains their immune systems.

It's OK If
I *Just* Dog Paddle?

A week after discharge, as I bring the hospital staff bagels and cream cheese, I continue to mull over the notion of doing a support group on oncology.

Nobody would know about the colostomy unless I speak of it. My agonizing fear over being horsefly bait like so much steamy roadkill is unfounded. The appliance is really state-of-the-art. The truth is I want others to know. How could I fail to disclose something that is such a part of me? It's my mission to normalize my condition, to dispel fear in others, and to tell them life can be so good after an ostomy. I have had some psychiatry patients who would rather die than consider a colostomy for Crohn's or cancer.

This is a disease of tradeoffs. To struggle with the "whys," to blame God, would keep me stuck in limbo without resolution. I work hard to find my stride in this self-confidence thing. (Years later, I would be able to enumerate all the positives that came with the experience, but I wasn't there at the time.)

In actuality, I've lucked out. I'm just going to have to become a champion hurdler.

Homecoming —I'm going to forego the Mrs. America pageant

today. I'm not up to the stroll down the runway, and I truly look about as ghastly as I feel. I haven't had my Wheaties in ages. My body is an insubstantial bag of nothing, and my psyche is in serious condition.

I obsess that the car airbags will deploy during the ride home and that I'll have to return to surgery.

The first thing I do once I'm home is to step on the scales, which at times have been my higher power. In a convoluted but female way (of which I'm ashamed), I think, "I'll deal with the cancer; just let me stay thin." I'm down 33 pounds from my slightly overblown fighting weight. I'm suffering emotionally but gloat that I can still fit another person into my old jeans.

The familiarity of home should be celebrated. But I'm on a bed of nails for all the comfort I find. The restlessness that I experienced in the hospital is magnified—from couch to chair to bed only to begin the drill again within minutes. I'm expending enough energy to fuel a small third-world country.

I figure that the culprit is a medication I'm taking for nausea. Finding confirmation in the "PDR" (Physician's Desk Reference, a compendium of medication information), I stop taking the pills and am able to relax.

While denying any "Pollyannaesque" musings, I do ascribe to a healthy dose of daily optimism. This guiding force in my life helps me to navigate the trouble spots, always believing "Why not expect the next good thing?" This allows me to acknowledge that the rough patches are only transitory and that joy is attainable if I choose it. With the "glass is half empty" philosophy, people fail to fully appreciate the good spells, dwelling instead on their fear about the next possible catastrophe.

Three days after I'm discharged, home health schedules a nurse visit to supervise things when I change the appliance. It's a clever combination of flexibility and efficiency, made of a miraculous material that sheds water, resists shifting due to friction, and adheres tightly to the skin (most of the time). It's dreadfully expensive for something that gets tossed out after 3 days, give or take.

I peel it off tremulously and squeeze out the paste that forms the leak-proof barrier. It's very gummy when I stick it to my belly, and I feel like I have half a dozen thumbs. It's scary being in the driver's seat for the first time, but I have a patient instructor.

Ten minutes after she leaves, she telephones panicky. "Did you throw out your trash yet? I've misplaced my tennis bracelet."

There it is in all its 14-carat beauty "smack dab" in the middle of my waste...how sublime!

Fifteen pounds of exuberant Siamese, poised, his hindquarters beginning to boogie, is ready to pounce and leap into my lap. He was so respectful last summer when my belly was healing. How could he forget so soon? I give him a real snoot full of that primeval smell of healing incision that only animal noses can detect, and he recoils as if I'd doused him with ammonia. "I love you too, Simon."

Anthropomorphizing him, I have often wondered if he was a nurse in a former life. He gazes at the "recovering me" with what I perceive of as such adoration.

Ever willing to nudge my ego, the children point out to me that Simon looks at the fleas in his luxurious fur with equal fascination.

Because my elimination has been shifted halfway around my equator, I think that whatever I ingest will exit much more quickly, like the whole process has been short-circuited. Doesn't happen; thankfully, I have yards of intestines to spare.

My older sister Linda arrives from Florida to nurse me back to some semblance of well–being. She is a vast comfort.

She is a bit alarmed by my appearance and says she can see through my skin —it has a bluish cast. Maybe it's just the aqua shirt I'm wearing, maybe not.

Nearly twins, we've had a lifetime of shared confidences. I can be honest with her without affectation. We stopped competing with each other years ago. NOT.

Shamefully, I take glee in the fact that I trounce her soundly in marathon Scrabble. I am still petty.

We go to the movies for a long-awaited "chick flick," dipping voraciously into the popcorn bucket. The thought of never being able to have buttered something again in this lifetime is more than I could have tolerated. Things are normalizing in my world.

I have a question that's been plaguing me, "When I get to heaven, will I be whole again?"

Linda says, "You are already whole, my Raine."

I cry as if my heart will break. And all of a sudden, I'm about five years old, and my sister is my champion, and everything will be right again. Historically, she's jousted with my scariest foes and chastised the bullies of the world just to defend me.

Basically, heaven is a place where I'll get to hug my grandmother again, where I'll be on a first-name basis with everyone I've wanted to meet, and I'll always get to go first class. Or, maybe I'll live in Paris forever and have plenty of time to see everything in the Louvre or stroll the Left Bank endlessly, discovering bargains at antique shops.

Anti-climactically, I get the news that the lymph nodes are clear and I have had "Stage One" cancer.

This is a big deal!!! Once again, I am able to avoid chemo or radiation. (The grocery list is extensive, but I still manage to go through the express lane.)

Next time I'm solo when I change the appliance thanks to some colossal snafu with managed care. Home health hasn't made a visit. I feel terribly abandoned, like someone's tossed me out of the lifeboat and there's a shark convention between land and me.

I'm overconfident and rush the process of positioning the appliance onto the stoma, not realizing the "poop shoot" is aimed upward in defiance of gravity!

The appliance is really "high tech." Once I overcome the fear that it will pop like a whoopie cushion if I exert myself or fill it with too much flatulence, I'm able to relax with some confidence. (I do remember an occasion when I took a flying leap onto a fat rubber inflatable only to have it pop loudly into flaccidity.)

For a while, I'm hypervigilant about odor or a leak or some calamity.

Feeling especially vulnerable to mishap one day, I try the sympathy game with Tom: "A baggie is all that stands between me and social embarrassment."

He reminds me that that is true for most people, except the usual barrier is underwear, which is far less reliable.

Polishing My *Stroke*

It is two weeks post-surgery, and I am returning to Dr. S's office to have my stitches and staples removed. Dr. Mc will be attending to me since Dr. S is on a well-deserved vacation cruising the fjords.

I'm relieved that Dr. Mc. chats face-to-face with me before the stitches are removed from my bottom. I interpret this as a classy move, given the realm of possible "conversational openers" for this type of procedure.

Oh bliss, I discover that I can sleep on my stomach again!

I am allowed to drive. Slowly all the little pleasures are possible.

Sadly, Kim Perrot, a Houston Comet, dies of brain cancer. All the love and prayers of family and fans could not save her. I am a member of the club now —their deaths a shared loss, their triumphs a shared victory.

I leave the room in tears. Something so gossamer connects my soul to yours that I will know you in Paradise.

Tom and I celebrate our 30th anniversary the next month with a jazz brunch at a favorite New Orleans-style restaurant. Quite magically, over Bananas Foster, I begin to flirt. His love makes me feel beautiful —like I'm 20 years old and about to be blindsided by that "look."

Tom is ardent —at 6 weeks I'm afraid to attempt a performance. What if I fail? My libido is in the cellar. Believing myself so diminished with this surgery, I find a hundred reasons why he should reject me too.

With a careful and devoted lover, I succeed, and my "mojo" works well. I cry with joy. Tom still thinks I'm a goddess —go figure.

After weeks of struggling with the unpredictability of elimination, I decide to "experiment" with irrigation. (Everyone tried to tell me it was preferable, but sometimes I'm pretty stubborn and like to do things my own way.) I figure I ought to be a pro by the time I'm released to go back to work in a week.

I learn the "knack" by being patient with myself, and about 95% of the time, it's a real success. It's self-contained and private. I have a comfortable fan chair with a plethora of plush cushions and can indulge in fabulous books or sewing projects while things empty out.

Instead of abhorring the process, I've learned to "embrace" it. This is a small accommodation in exchange for life.

I returned to work on my 52nd birthday. My co-workers give me a huge basket with more than ten pounds of assorted chocolate candies. My aversion to chocolate after surgery "one" didn't last long. I had begun to crave it again and feel compelled to demolish my cache relatively quickly.

"It's just not possible I'll ever have to battle the pounds again."

At the morning report on psychiatry, we get the "cast-iron stomach" lowdown on the highlights of the last 24 hours. Sometimes this includes a bit more about bodily functions than I care to hear. Word has it that an elderly gentleman on the unit has had a normal bowel movement after several days of constipation.

I smirk, "I'd be rather pleased about that myself."

And so I ease back into my world. I've really missed my "family."

Things in psychiatry are akin to a well-run M.A.S.H. unit. Circumstances are unimaginably sad, but often there is a huge helping of sheer absurdity thrown into the mix to keep staff reasonably healthy. I have grown immeasurably in this environment.

My sense of exuberance is not spoiled by a slight mishap. I'm sporting an ungainly arm brace. An agitated patient has upended a table that glances off my wrist. I brandish my injury and quip to my boss, Tony, "Thank God, I have something else to focus on now...I've milked the cancer about all I can. Ask my family."

The grieving still comes in waves. Just as winter is beginning to establish an austere hold on things, the dog dies. Missy was a 14-year-old terrier who had lived with us for many years.

She had simply gotten too small for her grizzled coat. Rescued from a shelter when my children were young, Missy would have been happy just to be loved (watering and feeding were simply extra pleasures). She was a reminder of happier family times before my children had to grapple with life and death issues.

So my tears for her contain the salt of many losses. I weep because I want to go back to that time. I want to have the experience of never having gotten cancer.

Sometimes, I want the old "me" back. But how can I go on wishing for the "me" that was dying by inches?

Yet, I'm truly afraid to live. I let the cancer define who I am, and I'm too quick to wear the mantle "I'm an invalid." I see life in terms of limitations and grieve the things I think I can no longer do.

So far, my list includes never wearing a bikini again (hasn't happened since my honeymoon) and never being able to sleep out in the wilds.

I confess to absolutely abhorring Girl Scout overnights and camping in the "great outdoors." All too often I'd had to contend with bugs of all sorts and a wet tarp floor and the sensation of having to pee again, though it hadn't been that long since I'd slogged off to the latrine.

Staying Afloat is *Too* Much Work

I am really a textbook case in manifesting the stages of grief as formulated by Elizabeth Kubler-Ross. I find myself mired in incredulity at times... did this really happen to me? This illustrates denial quite readily. It's as if nightmare becomes reality, but we're not ready to accept anything about it.

Anger holds me in its powerful grip. I find myself vacillating between gratitude and fury. Prolonged anger takes on a life of its own, crippling the mind. Transitory anger can be a powerful catalyst to evolve into a different, more comfortable place emotionally.

I was angry at God for a brief while before gaining perspective – a grasp of the "big picture." It wasn't God's fault... WHY NOT ME? Who was I to expect special dispensations?

As much as I try to rearrange the facts, the outcome is still the same. Bargaining is just an attempt to find somebody or something to blame for an adversity or, perhaps, to puzzle over a way to fix things as if we could erase what's been done. Somehow, we think we need to have that piece before we can move on.

A better example of this bargaining was illustrated by the press in the aftermath of Princess Diana's death in Paris in 1997. So much speculation rested on the "what ifs"…the driver hadn't been drunk; she had been wearing her seatbelt; the paparazzi hadn't been chasing her Mercedes into the tunnel…all of which didn't change a thing about the tragic outcome.

Depression becomes an albatross around my neck for many months. It was my effort to find meaning in my suffering that served to mitigate the pain.

Acceptance for me is about embracing life again after walking through the "valley of the shadow." I am not going to live my life according to the constraints of my grief. Anything is achievable if I choose to warp my mind around it.

It would be some time before I measured life by all I could still do.

Navigating managed care is a bit like walking through a field peppered with land-mines.

On the plus side, my bill for "room and board" alone, which nearly exceeded a year's pay for me (3 out of the 8 days being in ICU), was paid in full only because I worked for a "sister" hospital.

The "board" part, of course, didn't provide me with any filet mignons or lobsters and, what I eventually got for "regular diet," wasn't worthy of a "brown bag."

I can only speculate about all of the other charges accrued for the surgeon, the anesthesiologist, the pathologist, drugs and miscellaneous disposable items. Even a co-pay of 20% on such a sizeable bill would have been staggering.

But, here's the hitch…it's like this good news/bad news rubric… my policy will not reimburse me for the "durable medical equipment" (appliances, irrigation supplies and adhesives) I will use for the rest of my life. I begin a letter writing campaign protesting this issue and, eventually, I become successful in my quest. I feel like a pariah since the company readily pays for diabetic supplies.

It's Still Too Far *to* the Other End

Every day provides a lesson in living.

If I'm going to be hobnobbing with polite society, I avoid whole kernel corn. My digestion creates lots of gas, and I fire off like a machine gun. On a positive note, I can eat just about everything else, including ice cream, which used to give me cramps.

At times a phantom sensation, coupled with years of habit, convinces me I can sit down and take care of that uncomfortable fullness. I'm a quick study, but it will probably take years to erase this conditioning.

I have a "diarrhea" dress relegated to the back of my closet... too many negative vibes.

I'm convinced my therapy group attendees know what a disaster things are, but perhaps they really chalk it up to the fallout from some spicy food and don't realize I'm the offender. I perpetuate the charade by looking innocent, and I survive the experience after a quick trip home and a change of clothing.

For this reason, I never go anywhere without Imodium.

I met Dr. G, who is lauded as "one of the best" oncologists, according to my friend Betty, who had sought out a specialist to treat her ailing husband. I luck out again...Dr. G is wonderful. He's very thorough and kindly fields a variety of my rudimentary questions about follow-up. His office runs some labs —liver panel and CBC. Tests indicate that I am healthy.

I resist calling myself a cancer patient —it's like that hat with ear flaps that Mom forced me to wear. There was not a single thread of that head covering that suggested femininity. I can pretend it's not "me." What a bunch of malarkey! Like it or not, the label is mine.

At year's end, Tom and I manage a short stay in London. I slog through rain puddles and find that I've packed a pair of shoes that pinch my toes, but I'm still enamoured! There's a part of my heart I leave there with each visit, just for safekeeping.

Being your basic serfs, we do not manage an audience with HRH Elizabeth II but are ecstatic to see Vanessa Redgrave in a Noel Coward revival. She is magnificent and a true royal, if you ask me.

I take "parental" pride that my elimination works beautifully despite the reality that I am 6 time zones due east from home and my "routine."

I am very touched when I find out that Aunt Ruthie remembers me daily at the temple where she prays for Uncle Milton's repose. I am quite humbled by this and so many other kindnesses.

What a rare thing it is to step back from this experience and say, "Yes, I've dealt with it now, and I can move on and be happy."

I am asked to meet with two colostomy patients on the skilled nursing unit at the hospital. They are understandably terrified, uncertain about the future. I think I find myself pirouetting in front of them when they ask the questions that I asked all those months ago...can I go to church...can I wear pantyhose...will I have a life after cancer? Look at me, ladies!

I have pearls of wisdom that could really make a difference in the healing of other cancer patients, yet the doctors seem threatened by the presence of a "non-com" practicing in their rarified environs. The nurses enthusiastically welcome my presence, but the referrals do not come readily.

During my recovery, I would have so welcomed dialog with a survivor, someone who could wear form-fitting clothing and wasn't stinky and repulsive. I wanted to provide that reassurance to another. I feel that "I'm all dressed up with nowhere to go."

I must be vigilant with checkups. I must deal with that "specter" that sneaks up on you if you get too complacent and pinches you on the neck like a post-Apocalyptic beetle. I tend to replicate mutant cells, so that places me in a higher risk group for other cancers.

I begin to dream on occasion about the colostomy. In my meanderings, I find that it doesn't stop me from anything I've ever wanted to do. I am accepting.

There are exotic places that need exploring and so many books to be read. Today my somewhat reticent 17-year-old ambushes me with a hug that takes my breath away.

I take particular delight in my garden this spring. Things that lie fallow should be renewed. Where the land is scarred, beauty can flourish again.

I Need to Remember That I've Already Had Swimming Lessons

I am inspired at times to throw out thought-provoking questions.

This time, around a food-laden conference table at work, I ask of my colleagues, "Who were your childhood heroes?"

Standard stuff in return — Roy Rogers, the Mercury Seven, and Sir Edmund Hilary (a name I provided). I could have responded "my family," as trite as it sounds (like I'm a Miss America contestant sucking up to the judges). But this disclosure is not an affectation, it is genuine.

As intricate wood turnings are spun out on a lathe, my experiences —and the parenting I received—have shaped me to deal with adversity and, above all, celebrate happiness.

My parents remain vital and loving into their ninth decade.

I'm descended from good Puritan stock and the testament to their steadfastness is an ancestral home in Beverly, Massachusetts built in the late 1620s. It is touted as the "second-oldest wood-frame house" in America.

My parents have never wavered in their affection for me, despite the reality that they were both devastated by trauma in their formative years. They could well have let bitterness and the fallout from abandonment overwhelm their lives. They are individuals who have earned their wings while on earth.

My beloved grandmother, Alice, tragically died in her 39th year when my mother was only nine. In the harsh New England winters, she had developed "weak lungs," having inherited a tendency toward asthma. She was allergic to the only viable treatment of the time, a medicine derived from horse serum. My mother remembers the ambulance pulling up to the gates of Wood Lea to transport her mother Alice to the hospital—sadly, the very last time she would see her.

Winter being particularly hostile that year, my grandfather David and his children were all ill with throat and ear infections. Kindly townspeople offered to separate the family while David could recover mentally and physically from his personal holocaust, but he would not give his consent, fearing the separation would become permanent.

My father "lost" his father during the waning years of the Depression, when my grandfather—perhaps, suffering an amnesic episode —left his family, never to be seen again. He'd been a World War I veteran and returned stateside showing the ravages of "shell shock." My dear grandmother, Bessie, prompted by the mysterious circumstances of his departure, was forced to deflect suspicion away from herself by giving testimony to the authorities.

My parents met before World War II, as my mother, literally, waltzed into my father's life at a party given by mutual friends. They have been dancing together, without a misstep, for 60 years.

I had an idyllic and enviable childhood.

My only sibling, Linda, and I are separated by a mere 11 months. I can only imagine what havoc two babies brought to the staid farmhouse at Wood Lea, my maternal grandfather's property, where we lived until my parents were able to build their own house post-war.

When I was a child, nearly everyone on my street was related— some relationships more convoluted than others. There was always a listening ear in that New England, rural community. This speaks to a bucolic existence best depicted in beloved films like *"It's a Wonderful Life and A Christmas Story."*

With Linda, my co-conspirator always leading the way, I held on to my shyness for many years. I was always the observer as my sister plotted ways to experience the world— some, I'm sure, rather frightening for my parents. As soon as she perfected the breakout or planned the grand adventure, I became the follower. She was substance. I was shadow. She would initiate. I would imitate.

My paternal grandmother lived in New Hampshire in a compact bungalow, "sans garage" which was pulverized in the 193_ hurricane, despite my father's efforts to battle nature.

To this day, I think of my grandmother often. She must be one of the brightest stars in the firmament.

Her home lacked running water and a heating system, but it was a divine respite from the busy world beyond "Cricket Corner". Her kitchen was commanded by a behemoth of a cast iron stove. I can still remember the colors and shapes of her mixing bowls and what it felt like to master the hand pump that disgorged drinking water.

Best of all, there was a shed attached to the barn which served as bathroom facilities, albeit primitive. Cleverly, it was not "one size fits all" and could provide security for even the smallest bum. This served to diminish a childhood fear: "I'm going to fall in."

My father, in his youth, had decorated the outhouse walls with hand-drawn portraits of many of the voluptuous Hollywood starlets of the day. Although the shed has likely been razed by now, it could have been ensconced in the Smithsonian as an early 20th-century artifact.

In my grandmother's arms, pillowed by her ample bosom, I could feel deliriously safe.

Although my grandmother had been dead for many years by the time I gave birth to my daughter, I often mused about the role she must have played in choosing Rachel from among the precious babies in heaven awaiting birth. As if to mark her selection, my grandmother lovingly set a dimple into her chin—the baby version of her own.

At my grandmother's knee, I learned an appreciation of great literature and a desire to be "neighborly," to help others.

At Wood Lea, I found serenity among the gentle farm animals and developed a real reverence for the land. My grandfather cultivated the best apples in the State of Massachusetts and was a prognosticator for weather trends as published in "*The Yankee Magazine*" and "*The Farmers' Almanac.*" He was the consummate farmer.

Linda and I were delighted at milking time when a stray cat was treated to a squirt of milk, warm from the udder. We were always sure to give the bull a wide berth. I was photographed atop a cow once, riding her bony hips into the sunset.

The barn was a vast stage for performing our own dramas, costumed with rusty garments from an old leather trunk sequestered in a tack room. We managed to take great pleasure in raiding the cellars for the just-barely-ripe Mackintosh apples awaiting sale. As the sweet juice ran down my chin, I thought this fruit was absolutely glorious.

When lambs were born in the early spring—often with snow still on the ground—my grandfather, understanding the ways of nature, would walk the pastures searching for newborn foundlings rejected by their mothers. Barely viable and likely to die if unattended, these lambs were brought into the farmhouse kitchen to be revived in the bread warming oven of his cast iron stove. To our delight, my sister and I got to bottle feed these babies before school every day.

Childhood spats aside, my sister and I were tremendous buddies. We could, literally, play from dawn to dusk in the safety of our hometown. Our imaginations alone would make time interminable. Growing up then had a wonderful innocence sadly absent from today's world.

Despite times when money was a bit scarce, my parents always prioritized family vacations. Many a summer vacation was spent in the quaint villages of Cape Cod. I have stored away fond memories of lobster races, gleefully chasing them across the floors of the cottage as their splayed pincers clacked against the wooden planking. Less endearing was an effort to preserve a bucket of starfish for the trip home by secreting our stash beneath bunk beds.

Although my mother was a registered nurse on night duty at a nursing home, she happily sacrificed sleep to provide a nurturing experience for my sister and me. She assisted in leading a Girl Scout Troop; typically made all of our clothes (including tailoring sport coats for my father); sang in the church choir, and was an officer in the Eastern Star.

She remains an ideal to emulate.

My father undertook a college education at nearly forty. He was a draftsman whose blueprints achieved perfection, although the use of computers for this field were still years in the future. He was active in the Masons and the American Legion when membership in organizations was still at an all-time peak. He remains political to this day and writes prolifically and well.

My parents are deeply admired by family and friends.

My sister was barely viable at birth, my mother having been too heavily medicated while in labor, or so we thought. Years later, doctors would detect heart abnormalities, probably inoperable at that time because surgical skills hadn't advanced to that level.

She had her fourth major cardiac procedure several years ago. When her pulse dropped to a mere 30 per minute, she underwent pacemaker surgery to restore appropriate rhythm.

Fortunately, she flew to Massachusetts to enter a venerable heart institution for her surgery. Doctors there would not be intimidated with the scope of the procedure required. I have often speculated that one with such a "big heart," with limitless generosity and affection, could ultimately be handicapped by a physically underdeveloped organ. Surgeons literally had to rebuild one of the ventricles of her heart.

No one would ever know that modern technology is the very reason why she is alive today. She is truly selfless and one of my most fervent champions, a much nicer person than I am.

My son was diagnosed with Type I diabetes around his 23rd birthday. Being a psychotherapist, I had trained myself to expect some back-sliding on his part, a failure to take care of his condition adequately. How could I have underestimated his having the "right mettle?" Despite the seriousness of Chris' circumstances, I never noticed any lapses of self-pity. It was a day of tremendous jubilation when he undertook a running of the Houston Marathon and made a respectable finish barely 18 months into his illness.

I say now how very much I admire all of you. You have left an indelible impression upon my soul. You are my heroes.

Remembering to *Breathe*

A summer vacation in France is a beautiful respite, even though I pack extra antibiotics to knock out a nasty bladder infection.

I marvel that I have stamina galore, that I can canoe on the Dordogne with the best of them, and climb the 250 (and counting) stairs of the Arc de Triomph without breaking stride.

Wrapping up the vacation in Paris, we watch the last leg of the Tour de France and Lance Armstrong's stunning victory. I mentally telegraphed him a "C'est magnifique!" I don't want to confuse this with narcissism, but I think he can pick up on this though I am just one of thousands milling about on the Champs Élysées.

Being fairly well organized, it's not difficult for me to get irrigation timing things going. Ideally, it needs to be done every 24 hours, with a "window" of two hours either way.

Clearly, with my schedule, I choose the evening —who wants to wake at 5:30 every morning? With my routine, it's not disastrous if my colon is sluggish and won't empty in an hour. But if the catastrophe occurs on my one-hour commute, or while seeing patients, things could become tricky.

As happens on occasion, I do become constipated. Hydration is critical for things to work properly.

One time vacationing in Provence, after a rigorous day in the beating sun, I get poor results while irrigating. My system being fairly dehydrated, literally sucks up the water I introduce via irrigation without yielding any benefit. I am afraid to go to the dining room that evening for fear my intestines will misfire.

I never resort to stimulants to unclog things because they're too harsh. Occasional use of stool softeners works quite well.

It's August, and we're nudging in on an anniversary of sorts, and I'm scheduled for a repeat CT scan and chest films.

Just for good measure, my urologist thinks it's time for an IVP (kidney x-ray) and cystoscopy (urethral stenosis being a chronic and bothersome condition for me).

The thought of going into the surgical suite for the procedure prods my anxiety into overdrive—and, for the first time in months, I express fear about the state of my health.

I wait for the exam and dilation where I waited last year, thankfully getting some mild sedation before anxiety can raise my blood pressure to the ceiling.

It's a "quickie" and I'm back to outpatient recovery ready to crawl into a barcalounger to slough off the last bit of anesthesia. I'm so relieved and not beyond a bit of mischief when I see a stroller with a precious bundle parked just inside my doorway— "I didn't even realize I was pregnant..."

The snooze I have once home is one of those that mimic a coma, and afterward, when my wits return, I tear into a thick novel, relishing the fact that I have the rest of the day to loaf.

But early afternoon brings a telephone call from the oncology clinic nurse. There's something strange on the liver, and the office wants to order an MRI to further evaluate things. It's Friday, and someone has already pissed all over my weekend.

Using a perfect, noncommittal script, nurse Hatchet says, "I'm not ready to tell you that the cancer has metastasized... We're not going to panic yet."

By golly, I will if I want to! Her hit-and-run technique leaves me chilled.

There's a part of me that would just as soon not know what happens next. I fret and stew, and every morsel I ingest turns into battery acid once my saliva starts on it. I am mired in quicksand.

There's the mother of all electrical storms tonight. The gusts whip furiously at all the plants the summer's drought has spared. It's so fitting that nature has turned on itself too.

I have been scheduled for an MRI ASAP. Frustratingly, this means a ghastly wait of 8 days. Once again, I ask for some Valium to temper my over-active ruminations rather than lose myself to pity. The wait is shortened to 3 days with a well-timed cancellation.

How has cancer changed me? I might have expected this big epiphany like Moses getting the stone tablets down from Mt Sinai (I think that's a New York hospital anyway). Truthfully, I would never expect a "Burning Bush" or reports from the Middle East that the Red Sea had once again parted, but I do notice and glorify in the daily miracles that abound. My eyes haven't become jaded by life's calamities. Thankfully, I'm a hopeful person.

Mine has been subtler than these Biblical wake-up calls. I'm still dogged and a fighter, but I'm more "que sera sera" more gracious about letting life flow without interrupting it to suit my own selfish ends—a bit more serene on a daily basis.

But, apart from this resolve, I am terribly unnerved. Like a little girl, I curl up in Tom's lap, wanting to make myself invisible.

I feel like a marine animal that's been stranded on a beach. Outwardly, it's placid, but inside, things are absolutely willy-nilly like a crab with spindly legs nervously tattooing the sand of an empty tidal pool. The truth can be seen in the eyes.

Being cloaked in doom and gloom, I am just not echoing Tom's optimism now.

I am as dazed and confused as I would be years later standing on a subway platform in Tokyo staring in disbelief as I watch the closing doors of a car bound for Kamakura. I am "left in the lurch" by my fleet-footed family. Without money or passport, no sense of direction, and only an inkling of the location of our ryokan, I am truly pitiful.

How did I allow the skeins of this situation to unravel so badly?

I managed to clear my head with a good pee in one of those public, Japanese-style stand-up toilets and develop a plan of action. Luckily, the planets were aligned for a reunion with my family two stops away. Amid a sea of dark hair on the tram, Rachel spots my blond individuality and hastens me off the train.

A dozen or so pages ago, I gave my journal to Dr. S for review. It was a bit like sending my firstborn off to school and worrying he wasn't clean enough behind the ears, or that his nose was snotty, or maybe that he'd say something wise-ass to the teacher.

I'm a "good" patient. When I was in the throes of a rather protracted natural childbirth 28 years ago with Chris, I overheard the murmurings of the staff just outside my door: "She must have a high tolerance for pain." Not really—just not wanting to disgrace myself.

The MRI is casket-like with little clearance overhead. I have to peek, which really gets me in trouble. To cope, I get creative and spin a scenario in which I'm a NASA scientist being jettisoned from the mother ship on a classified mission.

Or, perhaps, I'm in pursuit of that elusive stash of kryptonite so Superman can be safe forever.

Anyway, this works for most of the time I'm encapsulated in the machine.

During the last phase of the test, I'm injected with dye—I guess to check for blood flow in those densities picked up in the CT. I practice deep breathing and holding it in while the machine pings and jackhammers away.

The next afternoon, Dr. G's nurse calls with minimal feedback —

the test indicated some abnormality at the dome of the liver, atypical of metastasis disease.

I think this is cause for a mini celebration, and all of a sudden, I'm ready to canonize nurse Hatchet!

I am referred for an ultrasound to rule out anything that may be significant.

I won't be wearing a bikini this year, but I'm going to keep on swimming.

I've followed the protocol for prepping but the technician rather cavalierly says I'm full of gas and that we need more sophisticated imaging to see through all the bubbles.

I luck out that a radiologist is on standby, and I have the verbal report immediately without having to endure all the usual red tape rigormorole and a "nail biting" wait of several days.

No abnormalities—just the fatty infiltrations expected of a liver in excess of 50 years, even a "well-cared-for" liver.

I return to Dr. G's office for more good news. My blood work is also indicative of healthiness. Nevertheless, there are reminders that the thread is tenuous. In the waiting room, there's a woman wearing a turban. It looks incongruously festive against her pale face.

Getting *Caught* in the Current

I have a friend who is dying of acute myelogenous leukemia. She has been brought home from the hospital to die. Not for a moment is she bitter and complaining.

I hold her hand and kiss her cheek and try to say goodbye, but she keeps things uplifting and in the moment. She teaches me about grace and tells me that she prays for my recovery. And I think it is the most precious thing anyone has ever done for me.

I watch with bewilderment. Her daughter, Katie, has all the detachment of a five-year-old as she sits absorbed in a cartoon at Laura's bedside.

A moth pastes itself against the window...it's all so fragile. I wonder, where is God in all this?

The "wanting you to fight harder" is really more about me, isn't it Laura?

At times I question my survival when others have not been lucky. That "survivor" guilt is a tough morsel to swallow. How did I avoid getting on the airplane that crashed?

I survive because God has work for me and it's simply not my time – that's the current philosophy. Even so, why does Laura have to lose her struggle?

"

The next fall I travel to the State Capitol to address the Medical Board. I have independent disclosures from two male patients that a well-known doctor—an avuncular sort, who had been practicing for many decades—was sexually abusive to his male patients over several generations. It's not fun to have to be a crusader but necessary according to the dictates of my licensure. Thankfully, the physician in question is suspended by the board and, can, hopefully, "do no more harm."

With the ugliness of 9/11 clouding my perspective, I decide to enroll in a watercolor class. It provides an oasis for me in the desert of world politics. I paint portraits even though my instructor tells me I am not ready. I take issue with that and rebel. It is a lovely way to give expression to my feelings.

I make a concerted effort to avoid the evening news. It's really just a witch's brew of bad events — clearly, I don't need more exposure to trauma.

I experience a crisis of faith and vulnerability at this time. I think seriously about pursuing my own therapy to work through these feelings. Once again, test results are inconclusive—CT scan, as well as mammogram—and there is little I can do about the panic that seeds a new crop of doubt.

Living near a National Guard installation where NASA pilots train, I am accustomed to the drone of aircraft overhead. But, this particular morning, so soon after the holocaust in New York and the East, I home in on the rumble with unusual misgivings. Am I to have no security—outwardly or inwardly?

The world is too scary...I feel victimized, swirling through an eddy, being carried to a cataclysm residing in the storm drain.

Tom's support never wavers. I do not take such a marvelous man for granted.

Sure and *Steady* Progress

I find it so incongruous that I am scheduled for a bone scan in the same week I'm attending a *Smashing Pumpkins'* concert. It is a routine, "let's rule out osteoporosis" kind of thing and the results are good.

At the concert venue, Tom and I get moshed around in the pit for a while and quickly decide to seek higher ground. For the most part, it is glorious.

I must say that I'm a shameless flirt at times. As my normal exuberance returns, I learn to graciously accept a compliment or two. Dr. S remarks that I grow more beautiful with each month that passes and that he is always eager to see me for these checkups. It is strictly curative and probably just blarney, but well received, nevertheless. He is one of those people who affirm that "all is right with the world" by their mere presence.

The Internet is posting a flight to Madrid for a ridiculously low number of frequent-flyer miles. Ever adventuresome, we book for the Christmas holiday. In Toledo our hotel has this wonderful seraglio— here I come—Moorish-style chamber with a step-down tub. It is a regal, not-to-be missed experience, so I indulge myself.

Whether it was the exotic, and spicy emollients or something else that remains elusive, I regrettably have a Chernobyl suntan around the stoma—and this in day-glow fiery hues.

Basically, after surgery that patch of skin might as well have been in North Dakota. It was a nerve regeneration kind of thing that convinced me that it was mine again.

I itch myself into a frenzy, like I did even after Mom warned me against scratching poison ivy blisters. Regrettably, the ecstasy was short lived when the appliance refuses to adhere to the ravaged skin. I've learned that skin integrity is a big deal. In the future I'll use a lighter touch and pace myself.

I remember the very last day I gave into tears. I become frustrated when people comment about how well I'm doing. I often feel my optimism is a sham.

How can I heal people if I'm having such a hard time healing myself?

As I often do, I found a revered sage in Sharon, who tells me that being grateful and being angry are not mutually exclusive. Several months of stored tears provides sufficient cleansing. As a good Quaker, she promises to "hold me in the Light."

One day at work, one of our most psychotic patients stops me in the hallway to inquire about my status. She prays over me, citing every deity known to man—and some of her own creation—as fervidly as any child who first comes to know God.

Profane at times and with a measure of mumbo jumbo, she credits herself for my clean bill of health as if the certainty of my recovery was a "no-brainer."

In Rome I have hit my stride in this confidence game. Several years out of the gate, I am no longer plagued by doubts about my condition. Hope has taken flower.

In St. Peter's Basilica, I request a blessing of an English-speaking priest. It was an experience to hold dear always.

In France in the fall of 2004, I lapse into a period of malaise—this in the aftermath of a misfortune in Nice. A thief has made off with all of our belongings.

Again the feeling of being damaged, that I am going to have to effect a miracle to round up new colostomy supplies. As Tom points out to me, this is one of the most heavenly places on earth to be in this dilemma. After all, the French do have colon cancer and sometimes have to deal with the unpredictabilities of colostomies. The hotel manager, sympathetic with our circumstances, gives us a room with a magnificent view of the Mediterranean and not the parking lot as we had booked.

We are directed to a surgical clinic to pick up said supplies by a kindly "docteur" where I am able to procure some "free" wafers and pouches that look doll-sized compared to those I usually order. Crisis at bay, I'm vastly appreciative. "C'est la vie."

I'm prone to a colostomy "Charley Horse" if I twist too rapidly or rise abruptly from a prone position. It feels like a have a kink in my slinky and takes my breath away.

Swimming Like An *Olympian*

I scan the lapis sky for birds...it is a "clear, you can see for miles," stellar day. They're out in force, skirting the static, muggy air close to the landing strip. Others scatter like confetti at higher altitudes.

I know now that it was all about faith. This is the day I will literally fly, though I have been metaphorically at it for several years now. My parents are here, as well as my sister, my husband and children, all eager for my first jump. My tiny granddaughter, Jenna, is also an observer. Linda takes the enviable position of copilot as the engines begin to sputter.

The twin otter takes us up to 14,000 feet before leveling off, and Eric (a VERY experienced jumper) and I toddle to the plane's doorway, trussed together as we are for a tandem sky dive. I am calmer even than I happened to be that last day, that I still had cancer nearly 5 years ago. This is the culmination of so much and would not have been possible but for my suffering.

My thoughts as we tilt into space are of heaven and of Dr. S., to whom I dedicate this jump. He was an extraordinary man whom I will forever miss.

Although I'm outwardly cool, I am uneasy when we begin the free-fall portion of the dive. I've left my stomach aboard. My hands chatter like castanets, trying to grab onto something solid to slow the decent.

After the drag shoot deploys, however, the ride is heavenly. It is so deliriously wonderful that I have become a bird, swooping and soaring to catch the thermals. We fall into God's embrace and have the most glorious time of it until our four feet touch down on terra firma.

It was a rare experience with a euphoria that has lasted for years.

Shortly after the jump, I return to work at the hospital to news that psychiatry is facing closure. Realistically, we'd been limping along for years trying to absorb the cost of the uninsured. Devastated as I am, I have a conviction that even this calamity is manageable. I call upon my fortitude and remind myself that change is opportunity. I begin to imagine this next productive and exciting phase of my professional life.

Six months ago, I had been approached by a colleague who is a physician's assistant in the T.H. Clinic. "Dr. W B is looking for a good therapist...what do you think?"

Now facing unemployment, I capitalize on that offer and open up my private practice, leasing space at the facility. Confidence in big business is at an all-time low for me, so the notion of self-employment sounds enticing.

And it has been. There are few places in the world where an office view can encompass so much: cruise ships docked at the pier, romantic horse and buggies pealing out the rhythmic jingle of bells; street cars sluicing along their tracks; and the Victorian architecture providing so much "eye candy."

I have become so content.

We can't change what's happened...all we can do is honor the past and move on with its lessons in our hearts.

Driving home over the Causeway recently, I make eye contact with a low flying pelican that seems to dip gracefully at my approaching car. His visage reflects a kind of prehistoric wisdom. The gulls overhead dance in the spume of a moving barge. Oh, God, what a privilege it is to share this magnificent earth with all of your creatures for this brief sojourn.